ANNAPOLIS
The Delaplaine
2021 Long Weekend Guide

Andrew Delaplaine

NO BUSINESS HAS PAID A SINGLE PENNY OR GIVEN _ANYTHING_ TO BE INCLUDED IN THIS BOOK.

I0151962

Gramercy Park Press
New York London Paris

Please submit corrections, additions or comments to
andrewdelaplaine@mac.com

ANNAPOLIS
The Delaplaine
Long Weekend Guide

TABLE OF CONTENTS

Chapter 1
WHY ANNAPOLIS?

If you're a history buff and like the feeling of "stepping back in time," you'll love Annapolis as it boasts more surviving 18th Century buildings than any other city in the United States.

Visitors to Annapolis experience a town that has changed very little since it was a Colonial seaport. Located at the mouth of the Severn River on the Chesapeake Bay, this historic city was the temporary capital of the United States from 1783-1784.

Architects and fans of historical architecture love Annapolis for its wealth of examples of Victorian and other 19th Century architectural styles including

Beaux-Arts, Colonial Revival, Tudor Revival, Craftsman, and American Foursquare styles of the 20th Century.

In 1966, the U.S. Department of the Interior named the historic downtown as the country's first National Historic Landmark District. In 2005, Annapolis was listed on the National Trust for Historic Preservation's Dozen Distinctive Destinations.

Annapolis was home to four signers of the Declaration of Independence. Signers William Paca, Samuel Chase, and Charles Carroll lived in Annapolis in 1776 while Thomas Stone moved to the city in the 1780s.

History buffs should know that the state capitol, built in 1772, is the oldest state capitol in continuous legislative use and is topped by the largest freestanding wooden dome in America. The 21-ton sarcophagus of John Paul Jones, known as the "Father of the United States Navy," is buried in a crypt beneath the sanctuary of the Naval Academy Chapel, which is open to visitors. Now, that's history.

Annapolis has a variety of interesting museums, most with historical themes, including the Maryland World War II Memorial. The **Banneker-Douglass Museum**, a museum documenting the history of African Americans in Maryland, is located in the historic Mont Moriah Church at 87 Franklin Street.

Preble Hall, named for Edward Preble who is known for his service in the War of 1812, houses the U.S. Naval Academy Museum.

Hammond-Harwood House, the grandest Colonial house in Annapolis, is considered the Jewel of Annapolis and contains an impressive collection of John Shaw furniture and Charles Willson Peale paintings.

The **Kunta Kinte** – Alex Haley memorial, located in downtown Annapolis, celebrates the place of arrival of Alex Haley's African ancestor, Kunta Kinte, a story told in Haley's book *Roots*.

The **Paca House and Garden**, one of Annapolis's most impressive restored 18th Century Georgian mansions, was built by William Paca, one of the signers of the Declaration of Independence mentioned above.

Theatre lovers visit Annapolis for its vibrant community theater scene that includes two venues in the historic district. **Colonial Players**, located on East Street, is a company that mounts productions on its small theater-in-the-round stage. During the Christmas season, Colonial Players produces a musical version of *A Christmas Carol*, first commissioned in 1981. **Annapolis Summer Garden Theatre** presents three shows a year on a stage that can be seen from the City Dock.

Boating enthusiasts know that Annapolis is the sailing capital of the United States (check out the sign announcing that fact located right before the Eastport Bridge). If you're without a boat you can take a 2-

hour cruise on the **Schooner Woodwind**, a beautiful 74-foot wooden schooner, departing four times daily from the dock at the **Marriott Hotel**. The Woodwind offers a hands-on experience allowing passengers to raise the sails, take the helm, watch for crab pots, and thoroughly enjoy Annapolis from the water. Boaters also love **Sandy Point State Park** where activities include boating, crabbing, fishing, swimming, and windsurfing. The Park also provides a great view of the Chesapeake Bay Bridge.

There's a great variety of dining options. The selection of specialty restaurants is impressive and there's something for every appetite. Fans of seafood should check out O'Leary's Seafood in Eastport (arguably the best seafood restaurant in the area) and **Cantler's Riverside Inn** (just 15 across from the Maryland State House of town). Joss Café, a locals' favorite, is known for the best sushi in town. For the best Chinese food, stop by **Nano's** on Main Street. For fine dining visit Harry Browne's across from the Maryland State House.

Shopaholics and those looking for special gifts will be pleased with the variety of shopping venues from specialty shops to antique shops. Of course Annapolis has all your favorite department stores with a good number of shopping districts including the **Westfield Annapolis** and **Arundel Mills** malls.

Antiques and one-of-a-kind collectibles are abundant in shops like **Evergreen Antiques, West Annapolis Antiques, Blue Crab Antiques.**

Annapolis's galleries feature ongoing collections of original art that will please both seasoned art collectors and the novice. Whether you're a history buff, antique shopper or nature lover, you'll find that Annapolis is a great day trip, but most discover that a Long Weekend is ideal.

VISITORS' CENTER
26 West St., Annapolis, 888-302-2852
www.visitannapolis.org
Has maps and lots of other useful information on tours.

Chapter 2
GETTING ABOUT

Once you're parked, you can easily get around on foot. Bikes are also an option.

CIRCULATOR. The city operates this free trolley that quickly and efficiently moves people from the city's 4 parking garages around the Central Business District, Westgate Circle to Memorial Circle. You'll see the signs.

Chapter 3
WHERE TO STAY

ANNAPOLIS INN
144 Prince George St., Annapolis. 410-295-5200
www.annapolisinn.com

This charming spot has only 3 suites and is near the City Dock and the Naval Academy. They have a superb collection of antiques, furnishings, and appointments. About as "Colonial" as you can get in very Colonial Annapolis.

ANNAPOLIS MARRIOTT WATERFRONT HOTEL
80 Compromise St., Annapolis. 410-268-7555
www.annapoliswaterfront.com/
This just-renovated hotel is the largest on the water and in the historic area. Treat yourself to a downtown hotel that combines modern elegance and convenience with Colonial charm. Well, the "Colonial" part might be a stretch, but this is a full-service property that, among other things, has rooms overlooking Chesapeake Bay, and others feature spectacular views of downtown Annapolis Harbor. (Rooms ending in numbers 6 through 31 have a water view.) the **Schooner Woodwind** sails from the dock here.

COUNTRY INN & SUITES CARLSON ANNAPOLIS
2600 Housley Rd., Annapolis. 410-571-6700
www.countryinns.com
Outside the historic district, but a free local evening shuttle is provided, based on availability. Indoor pool and fitness center; hot breakfast included; pets allowed.

GOVERNOR CALVERT HOUSE
58 State Circle, Annapolis, 301-261-2206
www.historicinnsofannapolis.com
The 51-room Governor Calvert House, located in one
of the oldest buildings in Annapolis, blends a bit of
history with modern luxury. Located in the Annapolis
Historic District, this hotel was the residence of two
former Maryland governors. The Calvert House
offers beautiful accommodations and amenities like:
high speed internet and cable TV. Conveniently
located steps away from the State House, US Naval
Academy, St. Johns College and the Chesapeake Bay.
A smoke-free hotel.

HISTORIC INNS OF ANNAPOLIS
58 State Circle, Annapolis, 410-263-2641
www.historicinnsofannapolis.com

Here you'll get to experience 18th century charm and history blended with 21st century convenience. They have 3 distinct hotels in downtown offering a refreshing mix of Victorian charm and modern conveniences. Each of their beautifully restored boutique hotels celebrates a place in American history.

THE MARYLAND INN
58 State Circle, Annapolis, 410-263-2641
www.historicinnsofannapolis.com
One of the oldest inns in Maryland, this Inn has welcomed Presidents, Governors and statesmen, including eleven delegates from the 1786 US Congress. Spanish Admirals were held prisoner at the Inn in 1898. All 44 rooms of this charming boutique hotel celebrate the Colonial splendor but have been modernized for the comfort of the guests and restored

with Victorian-era reproductions. The Inn contains a Starbucks, **Treaty of Paris** Restaurant and the Drummer's Lot Pub. Amenities include: flat screen TVs, and complimentary WiFi.

ROBERT JOHNSON HOUSE
58 State Circle, Annapolis, 301-261-2206
www.historicinnsofannapolis.com
This 29-room historic house overlooks the State House and Governor's Mansion. Built in 1773, today the Georgian style Inn offers elegantly-appointed accommodations with guestrooms that are furnished with beautiful 19th century antiques and period reproductions. Amenities include: high speed internet, cable TV and Fitness center.

THE WESTIN ANNAPOLIS
100 Westgate Circle, Annapolis, 410-972-4300
www.marriott.com

225 rooms in this Westin property, a big boring block of a building, but nice inside. Has all the usual amenities. Pool, fitness center, cocktail hours canapés, a nice touch. The **Azure** restaurant here offers a Continental menu along with some local favorites: smoked chicken tacos with avocado, pico de gallo, sour cream; Wings (buffalo or jerk); BBQ beef bites slow cooked and presented in beef brioche sandwiches; Falafel with cucumber, tomato, red onion, and spicy dipping sauce; Hummus served with grilled flatbread and vegetables.

Chapter 4
WHERE TO EAT

BOATYARD BAR & GRILL
400 Fourth St, 410-216-6206
boatyardbarandgrill.com
CUISINE: Seafood
DRINKS: Full Bar

SERVING: Breakfast, Lunch, & Dinner
PRICE RANGE: $$
NEIGHBORHOOD: Eastport
Nautical-themed eatery with a seafood focused menu.
Lots of bric-a-brac and photos cover the walls and
shelves above the tables. The cathedral style ceiling
has bright natural colored wood, just like all the other
wood in the place, which, combined with all the
windows looking outside, gives the place a bright
cheerful feeling. You'll see lots of Naval Academy
cadets in here, drawn (like the locals) by the high
quality and simply prepared seafood and the
reasonable prices. Also serving burgers and pizza.
Known for their Crab Cakes. Favorites: Maryland
crab soup and Soft shell crab. Reservations
recommended.

CANTLER'S RIVERSIDE INN
458 Forest Beach Rd., Annapolis. 410-757-1311
www.cantlers.com
CUISINE: Seafood
DRINKS: Full Bar
SERVING: Lunch & Dinner
PRICE RANGE: $$$
One of the best seafood restaurants in the area, and
some even say it's one of the best in the country. Well
worth driving or cabbing the 15 minutes outside town
where you'll find it tucked along the backwaters of
the Chesapeake Bay. You can arrive by boat or car.
It's a little tricky to find by car, so get detailed
directions from their web site and follow them
closely. Cantler's is an authentic "Maryland Family
Style" seafood restaurant where you sit at park

benches and eat shoulder to shoulder with everybody else. Steamed crabs are a favorite but so are lots of local, fresh-caught seafood choices. Cantler's is an Annapolis family-run institution. Try their soft crab sandwich, which is a whole crab with shell and an all but very soft and very delicious.

CARROL'S CREEK CAFÉ
410 Severn Ave, 410-263-8102
www.carrolscreek.com
CUISINE: Seafood/Steakhouse
DRINKS: Wine & Beer
SERVING: Lunch & Dinner
PRICE RANGE: $$$
NEIGHBORHOOD: Marina
Upscale white tablecloth waterfront eatery (dramatic setting overlooking the marina) featuring classic Chesapeake fare. Favorites: Inside, there's a nice bar where you can have drinks and maybe get some raw bar items (displayed on ice behind the bar). A perfect place to sit outside and watch the sun go down over the marina. Baked mini brie; Herb Encrusted Rockfish Fillet; Baked oysters with house-made bacon and Cheddar; Cioppino—their take on this classic dish comes with mussels, fish filet, clams, scallops, shrimp and an excellent tomato basil broth I haven't seen in years. For a great dessert, get the bread pudding with dark raisons & bourbon. Popular happy hour.

CHICK & RUTH'S DELLY
165 Main St. Annapolis. 410-269-6737
www.chickandruths.com

CUISINE: Delis, Bakery
DRINKS: Beer & Wine Only
SERVING: Breakfast, Lunch & Dinner
PRICE RANGE: $$
This place is as popular with locals as it is with tourists. They have a quaint custom of reciting the Pledge of Allegiance each morning. (Quick: do you remember all the words?) Big overstuffed sandwiches, creamy milkshakes.

DAVIS PUB
400 Chester Ave., Annapolis. 410 268-7432
www.davispub.com
CUISINE: American
DRINKS: Full Bar
SERVING: Lunch & Dinner
PRICE RANGE: $$
This is about as pubby as you could wish. There's a tiny front porch for outdoor eating, Daily specials, sandwiches and crab cakes.

DOCK STREET BAR & GRILL
136 Dock St, 410-268-7278
www.dockstreetbar.net
CUISINE: American Traditional
DRINKS: Full Bar
SERVING: Lunch & Dinner
PRICE RANGE: $$
NEIGHBORHOOD: Naval Academy
Located in the former city jail, you can't miss this two-level tavern with its in-your-face exterior painted a commanding blue color. Rough-hewn brick walls inside and the dim lighting give the place a cozy,

almost confined atmosphere (like jail, I guess).
Behind the curved bar are a few TVs, so this is a good place to catch a game. Has the kind of bar grub you'd expect to find in Annapolis, Chesapeake Bay specialties like Crab cakes; a few salads, quesadillas, chicken wings, etc. The crab & corn chowder is very nice. They offer a "build your own pizza" that's cheap and good.

DRY 85
193B Main St, 443-214-5171
www.dry85.com
CUISINE: American (New)
DRINKS: Full Bar
SERVING: Lunch & Dinner
PRICE RANGE: $$
NEIGHBORHOOD: Downtown
Modern twist on a Prohibition-style speakeasy. This place has got to be one of the darkest bars I've ever been in. Thankfully, lights are strategically placed beneath the bar and over the booths against the wall, so there's light, but it's the darkness of the wood that makes the place so strangely enticing. Come here for the drinks (the bourbon bar has top-shelf bourbons you won't find anywhere else in Annapolis) but there's also a menu of better-than-expected American comfort food: charcuterie boards; fried pickles; wings; hand-cut potato chips; excellent selection of burgers, with my favorite being the blue cheese with fig. A couple of main plates are very good—the pork osso buco; and the slow-roasted pork ribs.

GALWAY BAY

63 Maryland Ave, 410-263-8333
www.Galwaybaymd.com
CUISINE: Irish
DRINKS: Full Bar
SERVING: Lunch & Dinner
PRICE RANGE: $$
NEIGHBORHOOD: Downtown
The plants overflowing from the flower boxes above the entrance give the place a definite European feel. Red-brick walls holding up a dark-beamed ceiling and high polished woods give a cozy feel to this Irish pub offering a menu of classic Gaelic grub and American standards. Favorites: Shepherd's Pie; Charred Orange Honey Salmon; a big selection of burgers; corned beef poppers; short ribs; all day Irish breakfast (Irish sausage, black and white pudding, and the rest). Impressive list of Irish whiskeys.

HARRY BROWNE'S RESTAURANT

66 State Cir., Annapolis. 410-263-4332
www.harrybrownes.com
CUISINE: American
DRINKS: Full Bar
SERVING: Lunch & Dinner
PRICE RANGE: $$$
Menus changes with the seasons in this fine dining establishment with its white linen service. Mushroom bruschetta, roasted beet salad, roasted quail, seared scallops. Lovely atmosphere.

JALAPENO'S

85 Forest Plz, 410-266-7580

http://jalapenosonline.com/
CUISINE: Mexican
DRINKS: Full Bar
SERVING: Lunch & Dinner, Dinner only on Sundays
PRICE RANGE: $$
NEIGHBORHOOD: Annapolis Towne Center
The fanciful wall murals and wall decorations help to give the place a slightly Spanish look, but it's the food that puts it over the top, making it a locals' favorite. They have both Spanish & Mexican menus, with a HUGE tapas menu covering a couple of dozen items. I'm always suspicious of menus that seem to offer "too much," but nothing I ordered here was less than very good. Favorites: Steak & chorizo fajitas; Chicken and shrimp fajitas. From the tapas menu: Artichoke hearts sautéed in olive oil & Serrano ham and topped off with sherry; Mussels sautéed in white wine & garlic. Delicious frozen margaritas. Kids' portions available.

JOSS CAFÉ
195 Main St., 410-236-4688
www.josssushi.com
CUISINE: American
DRINKS: Full Bar
SERVING: Lunch & Dinner
PRICE RANGE: $$$
The "in the know" sushi spot in Annapolis. They don't take reservations in this small place. (They don't have to.) Go to **Nano's** for Chinese food but stick to Joss for sushi. Has a nice outdoor patio.

LEWNES' STEAKHOUSE
401 Fourth St., 410-263-1617
www.lewnessteakhouse.com
CUISINE: Steakhouse
DRINKS: Full bar
SERVING: Dinner
PRICE RANGE: $$$

The Lewnes family has been serving fine food at this location since 1921.

Ordinary "choice" and "selected" beef comes from open grassland ranges. U.S. Prime steers, however, are selected from sources such as 4-H clubs, and Future Farmers of America where the animals are pampered and cared for on an individual basis. At the proper time they are shipped to cool weather feed lots in the upper Midwest where they are fed a special mash of oats, barley and wheat. During the last six weeks, the steers are fed a diet of corn to enhance fat marbling. This marbling provides flavor, tenderness, and juiciness for which U.S. Prime beef is known. Finally, the beef is aged under controlled conditions to enrich its flavor. But that's not all: It takes special broiling equipment to properly prepare the steaks. Here the get it up to 1800 degrees. They sear in the flavorful juices while browning the outside.

LEVEL SMALL PLATES LOUNGE
69 West St., Annapolis. 410-268-0003
www.lannapolis.com
CUISINE: American
DRINKS: Full Bar
SERVING: Dinner
PRICE RANGE: $$
Food here is obtained locally whenever possible.
They even list the farms they buy from on the menu.

Like Gorman Farm for produce, Fire Fly Farms for goat cheese. Bison and bacon sliders are a standout. Also their artisan charcuterie boards. Unusual items here you won't find on other area menus like chorizo dip, a flatbread topped with their own chorizo, garlic and Parmesan. High ceilings, but the warm earth tones make the room quite cozy.

LIGHT HOUSE BISTRO
202 West St, 410-424-0922
www.lighthousebistro.org
CUISINE: American Traditional
DRINKS: Full bar
SERVING: Breakfast, Lunch, Dinner,
PRICE RANGE: $$$
NEIGHBORHOOD: Naval Academy
The plain red brick building it's located in doesn't do the place justice. Inside, however, there's a lot of atmosphere created by clever design elements. Rough wooden boxes of various shapes mounted on the walls give it a rustic ambience, helped along by the old-style red brick walls with blond wooden accents. This upscale bistro is located in a restored shelter, offering a modern twist on America classics. Popular brunch spot. Favorites: Crab Gazpacho; Pulled chicken salad is excellent; Crispy Chicken & Coconut Risotto and You-Asked-for-It-Meatloaf.

MISS SHIRLEY'S CAFÉ
1 Park Pl, 410-268-5171
www.missshirleys.com
CUISINE: American Traditional
DRINKS: Full Bar

SERVING: Breakfast & Lunch
PRICE RANGE: $$$
NEIGHBORHOOD: Naval Academy
Cozy chain eatery offering a menu of creative
American comfort food. Popular brunch spot.
Favorites: Stuffed French toast and Crab Happy
Chesapeake Chicken Sammy (Crab cakes, chicken
and Fried egg sandwich). Menu changes every 6
months.

NANO'S
189 Main St., Annapolis: 410-267-6688
www.nanoasiandining.com
CUISINE: Asian Fusion
DRINKS: Full bar
SERVING: Daily lunch and dinner
PRICE RANGE: $$
For the best Chinese food, stop by Nano's on Main
Street. They have the longest sushi bar in Annapolis,
an authentic tatami room for private dining, and it's
decorated with artwork from local artists.

O'LEARY'S SEAFOOD

310 Third St., 410-263-0884

www.olearysseafood.com

CUISINE: American

DRINKS: Full Bar

SERVING: Dinner

PRICE RANGE: $$

Consistently highly ranked seafood spot in Eastport, this place is usually the first stop I make when I get to town. I start with the quickly fried oysters, among the best I've ever had. There's a lump crabmeat starter that's different: it's mixed with a Spanish style vinaigrette that creates a wonderful dish. You'll want to avoid the steaks and chops and focus solely on the fresh fish available the day you are here.

OSTERIA 177

177 Main St, 410-267-7700

osteria177.com

CUISINE: Italian/Mediterranean
DRINKS: Full Bar
SERVING: Lunch & Dinner-Tues - Fri, Dinner only
on Sat, Sun, & Mon.
PRICE RANGE: $$$
NEIGHBORHOOD: Historic District
The chairs upholstered in white fabric offer a stark
contrast to the dark walls and high ceilings painted
black. A few of the white tableclothed topped tables
look out on Main Steet, making it fun to sit and watch
all the activity going on outside. Otherwise, you're
inside the darker, elegant room. Modern twist on
Northern Italian fare. Excellent pastas. Favorites:
sushi-grade ahi carpaccio; Linguine alle Vongole and
Salmone alla Mugnaia. Excellent wine list.

PUSSER'S CARIBBEAN GRILLE

80 Compromise St. Annapolis. 410-626-0004
www.pussersusa.com
CUISINE: Caribbean, Seafood
DRINKS: Full Bar
SERVING: Breakfast, Lunch & Dinner
PRICE RANGE: $$
Fronting the marina is this place offering not just seafood using Maryland recipes, but Caribbean ones as well. Great place for drinks and meals day or night because the marina is so picturesque.

ROMANO'S MACARONI GRILL

178 Jennifer Rd, 410-573-1717
www.macaronigrill.com
CUISINE: Italian
DRINKS: Full Bar
SERVING: Lunch & Dinner
PRICE RANGE: $$
NEIGHBORHOOD: Parole
Local outpost of Italian chain featuring an open kitchen. Walls look like they're made of rough-cut stone from someone's yard, throwing off a very rustic Italian countryside feel, with numerous archways leading into the different rooms enhancing that impression. Still, it has a very "corporate" feel underneath everything. Great selection of brick-oven pizzas and pastas. Favorites: Shrimp Portofino and Fettuccine Gorgonzola (spinach, crispy prosciutto, mild gorgonzola sauce). Good if you have a crowd and want to keep the tab under control, so it's popular with families and weekend brunch. (Which is why I avoid the place on the weekend.)

RUTH'S CHRIS STEAK HOUSE
301 Severn Ave., Annapolis, 410-990-0033
www.ruthschris-annapolis.com
CUISINE: Steakhouse
DRINKS: Full bar
SERVING: Dinner
PRICE RANGE: $$$
As founder Ruth Fertel used to say, "If you've ever
had a filet this good, welcome back." And she wasn't
necessarily speaking with her tongue in her cheek.

THE SEVERN INN
1993 Baltimore Annapolis Blvd., Annapolis, 410-
349-4000
www.severninn.com
CUISINE: American, Seafood
DRINKS: Full bar
SERVING: Mon – Sat lunch and dinner; Sunday
brunch and dinner
PRICE RANGE: $$$
Located at the eastern side of the Naval Academy
Bridge, the Severn Inn provides panoramic views of

Annapolis, the Naval Academy as well as the Severn River. Has the usual Maryland specialties one comes to expect in this area, but also Lupe's Salvadorian Seafood Stew, which I like: crab, clams, mussels, lobster, tomatoes, cilantro, garlic served with steamed rice. The steals are notable, but don't ignore the sides like fried green tomatoes and the sautéed mushrooms.

SOUL
509 S Cherry Grove Ave, 410-267-6191
www.soulannapolis.com
CUISINE: Southern/American (New)
DRINKS: Full Bar
SERVING: Lunch & Dinner, Sunday Brunch, Closed Mondays
PRICE RANGE: $$
NEIGHBORHOOD: Downtown
Comfortable (the chairs at the bar are especially comfy) eatery with bare metal chairs and simple wooden tables in a medium-sized room with floor-to-ceiling windows looking out onto the street. There's a good bit of seating outside on the patio, so try that if the weather suits. Serves up modern takes on undeniably delicious Southern cuisine (and has some very nice small plates). Favorites: Deviled eggs with country ham; Cornbread with sweet pepper jam; Fried chicken sliders; Roasted oysters with hot pepper bacon butter; Hot Dixie Chicken; Memphis-style Baby Back Ribs. Weekend brunch.

VIN 909 WINECAFE
909 Bay Ridge Ave, 410-990-1846
www.vin909.com

CUISINE: American (New)/Pizza
DRINKS: Beer & Wine
SERVING: Lunch & Dinner- Wed – Sat, Dinner only
Sun & Tues, Closed Mondays / No reservations.
PRICE RANGE: $$
NEIGHBORHOOD: Eastport
Cottage-like restaurant (no reservations, so come
early) offering a farm-to-table menu of New
American cuisine in an old seaside-style bungalow
just dripping with charm. Clear-stained reclaimed
wooden floors remind you that this was someone's
house. Chairs at the kitchen bar allow you to look into

their exhibition-style kitchen, although the glass
partition dividing you from the kitchen is a major
distraction. Major. There is a much better wine bar

nearby which is where I prefer to sit. There's a picket fence surrounding an outside seating area. When I say they are a farm-to-table eatery, I'm serious. They even list all their purveyors, showing how proud they are about their sources. (I wish everybody did this—it would clear out a lot of restaurants in five minutes!) Delicious pizzas and vegetable dishes, meticulously hand-crafted. Favorites: Blue Crab Tower and Cast-Iron Skirt Steak. Impressive wine list. (Since they don't have liquor, it has to be.)

Chapter 5
NIGHTLIFE

49 WEST COFFEEHOUSE, WINEBAR & GALLERY
49 West St, Annapolis, 410-626-9796
www.49westcoffeehouse.com
This is only a block west of **Rams Head Tavern**.
Live classical, jazz, and folk music nightly.

ARMADILLO'S
132 Dock St, Annapolis, 410-280-0028
www.armadillosannapolis.com
Live entertainment ranges from jazz to blues to funk
as well as classic rock, acoustic rock, and oldies.

JAZZ AT THE POWERHOUSE
126 West St, Annapolis, 410-269-0777
Next to the **Loews Annapolis Hotel** they offer music the fourth weekend of every month.

MCGARVEY'S SALOON & OYSTER BAR
8 Market Space, Annapolis, 410-263-5700
www.mcgarveysannapolis.com
McGarvey's doesn't have live music, but draws a crowd for its oysters and beer. It even has its own private-label Aviator Lager. The place is loud, friendly and fun.

O'BRIEN'S STEAKHOUSE
113 Main St, Annapolis, 410-268-6288
www.obriensoysterbar.com

DJs play in this busy place near the Dock Thursday through Sunday from 10.

RAMS HEAD ON STAGE
33 West St., Annapolis, 410-268-4545
www.ramsheadtavern.com
One of the busiest venues for live music acts like Yacht Rock Revue, Big Bad Voodoo Daddy, Eddie Money, Gerald Albright, John Mayhall, Willie Nile & Dan Bern, Mason Jennings, Martin Sexton. Over 21. Cover charge applies.

Chapter 6
WHAT TO SEE & DO

ANNAPOLIS SUMMER GARDEN THEATRE
143 Compromise St., Annapolis: 410-268-9212
www.summergarden.com
The group offers 3 shows a year on a stage that can be
seen from the City Dock. In 1965, "Olde Town"
Annapolis had been designated a Registered National
Historic District, and restoration of many of its
historic buildings was just beginning. The following
year a group of arts enthusiasts, led by Joan Baldwin,
incorporated Annapolis Summer Garden Theatre

(ASGT) to give actors and theatre artists the opportunity to perform in the summer when other local groups were, generally, on hiatus.

BANNEKER-DOUGLASS MUSEUM
84 Franklin St., Annapolis: 410-216-6180
www.bdmuseum.maryland.gov
This museum documents the history of African Americans in Maryland. It's located in the historic Mont Moriah Church on Franklin Street. Named for Benjamin Banneker and Frederick Douglass, it's dedicated to preserving Maryland's African American heritage and serves as the state's official repository of African American cultural artifacts. The museum was dedicated on February 24, 1984. The Victorian-Gothic structure was included in the Annapolis Historic District in 1971 and placed on the National Register of Historic Places in 1973. The recently completed BDM is a four-story addition which uses the 19th Century brick of the church's north facade as its interior lobby wall.

COLONIAL PLAYERS
108 East St., Annapolis: 410-268-7373
www.thecolonialplayers.org
This company mounts productions on its small theater-in-the-round stage. During the Christmas season, they produce a musical version of "A Christmas Carol," first commissioned in 1981. Colonial Players offers a wide variety of dramatic productions in the heart of downtown Annapolis. Founded in 1949 by a group of Annapolitans dedicated to bringing high quality theater to what was

then a very small town on the Chesapeake Bay, the theater continues to thrive with a dedicated corps of volunteers and a loyal subscriber base. I highly recommend that you check their site to see what's playing during your visit.

HAMMOND-HARWOOD HOUSE
19 Maryland Ave., Annapolis: 410-263-4683
www.hammondharwoodhouse.org
Hammond-Harwood House is the "Jewel of Annapolis," certainly the grandest Colonial house in the historic town, preserved intact since 1774. In addition to its magnificent, perfectly preserved architecture inside and out, this National Historic Landmark contains an outstanding collection of John Shaw furniture and Charles Willson Peale paintings. Walk-in tours Tuesday-Sunday, noon to 5.

KUNTA KINTE
Annapolis City Docks, 443-852-7784
www.kuntakinte.org
The Alex Haley memorial, located in downtown Annapolis, celebrates the place where Alex Haley's African ancestor, Kunta Kinte, landed in America, a story told in Haley's bestselling book, "Roots," which was adapted to the widely popular 1977 television miniseries of the same name. Kunta Kinte was one of 98 slaves brought to Annapolis aboard *Lord Ligonier* in 1767. The site is now memorialized with a statue of Alex Haley.

JONAS GREEN PARK

2001 Baltimore Annapolis Blvd, Annapolis. 410-222-6141

www.aacounty.org/locations-and-directions

Located on the Severn River, Jonas Green Park offers a sandy beach for boat launching. The park hours are from dawn to dusk with the exception of the fishing pier which is open 24-hours a day for fishing only. Visitors must be actively fishing on the pier when in the park between dusk and dawn, as opposed to hanging out and doing drugs, let's say. Follow this link to view additional information about fishing in the parks.

Jonas Green, printer and newspaper editor, was born on December 28, 1712, in Boston, the fifth of the seven children. The Greens were a family of printers who came from Somerset, England, in 1627 to settle the colony of Massachusetts. Jonas Green learned the printing craft from his father, was employed by a Boston firm, and worked as a printer's apprentice in Philadelphia for his cousin Benjamin Franklin. In 1738, Jonas married and moved to Annapolis, where the General Assembly approved legislation appointing him the colony's public printer. Jonas Green served as public printer for the remainder of his life and as publisher of the revived Maryland Gazette from April 1745. Green served as a vestryman and registrar for St. Anne's Episcopal Church, city alderman, postmaster, and secretary of the local Masonic lodge, and belonged to the Tuesday Club of Annapolis, from 1745 to 1756. In addition to his titles of "Poet Laureate" and "Master of Ceremonies," club records refer to Green as "Jonas Green, P.P.P.P.P," for "Poet, Printer, Punster, Purveyor and Punchmaker general." Green died on April 7, 1767.

MARITIME MUSEUM
723 2nd St, Annapolis, 410-295-0104
www.amaritime.org
HOURS: Thurs – Sun; 11 am – 3 pm
ADMISSION: Free
Riverfront museum (formerly the city's last oyster packing plant) devoted to the ecology, maritime history & arts of the Chesapeake. Overlooking the Chesapeake Bay, this museum offers an interactive experience that celebrates the oyster and the maritime history of Annapolis. Boat tours available.

MARYLAND STATE HOUSE

100 State Cir, Annapolis, 410-946-5400
https://msa.maryland.gov/msa/mdstatehouse/html/home.html
HOURS: Open daily
Completed in 1779, the State House was the location of many historic events including George Washington's resignation as commander in chief of the Continental Army. The Continental congress convened here in 1783. The current state legislature meets here for an annual 90-term. Private and self-guided tours available.

NATIONAL CRYPTOLOGIC MUSEUM
FT. GEORGE G. MEADE

8290 Colony Seven Rd, Annapolis Junction, 301-688-5849
www.nsa.gov/about/cryptologic_heritage/museum
Open daily except Sunday
A few miles outside Annapolis
"Keep sending me the letters from the Archbishop of Silesia sent from Rome to Dresden. The key has been found here so that they can be read just like ordinary writing. But it is necessary to let them continue on their way while copying them exactly."

While these are the words of Napoleon writing to his son, the sentiments, and the games that nations play, have remained much the same. The letter above and much more can be found at the National Cryptologic Museum in Maryland.

Opened in December 1993 to much public enthusiasm, the museum, one of the few museums dedicated to the Intelligence Community (the spy museum being one of the others), it covers the history of the National Security Agency's Cryptology Department as well as America's cryptology history and legacy.

The museum is located, appropriately, hidden away in the woods and next to the NSA, where much of today's cryptology work is done. Among the many curious objects are a voice-encrypting phone used by numerous Presidents, reconnaissance satellites from the 1960s, and the gem for cryptologist enthusiasts an incomparable library of declassified books on cryptology, and original texts including Johannes Trithemius's Polygraphiae published in 1518.

Museum visitors can also examine such famous machines such as the ENIGMA Uhr created by the Germans to make codes during WWII -- and famously decrypted by Alan Turing -- as well as the TUNNY Cryptographic Machine sometimes referred to by the German military as Geheimschreiber, which can be translated into "secret writer" or "private secretary."

The museum also features a NSA Hall of Fame exhibit as well as exhibits dedicated to women and African-Americans who made significant contributions to cryptologic history. Along with the museum there is an extensive library featuring photographs, catalogs, and other articles relating to cryptography and cryptology.

Museum Gift Shop

The NSA Civilian Welfare Fund Gift Shop, located within the National Cryptologic Museum, offers a variety of merchandise ranging from unique NSA logo items to books and videos relating to the art and science of cryptology. **Gift Shop hours are 10:00 a.m. - 3:30 p.m., Monday through Friday; and 10:30 a.m. - 1:30 p.m., the 1st and 3rd Saturdays of each month.**

Adjacent to the Museum, is the <u>National Vigilance Park</u>. The park showcases two reconnaissance aircraft used for secret missions. The RU-8D serves to represent the Army Airborne Signal Intelligence contribution in Vietnam and the C-130 memorializes an Air Force aircraft that was shot down over Soviet Armenia during the Cold War.

NAVAL ACADEMY TOUR GUIDE SERVICE

Enter on Prince George Street or Randall Street
Armel-Leftwich Visitor Center, Annapolis. 410-293-8112

www.usnabsd.com/for-visitors

Park and walk onto the grounds at Gate 1; photo ID required for ages 16 and over.

Academy main page:

www.usna.edu

Main Chapel, Crypt of John Paul Jones, Public Tour in Bancroft Hall. Visit the United States Naval Academy in Annapolis, MD. Tour the historical sites and see history in the making as the Navy trains its future generations of officers. Take a guided walking tour of the Academy with professional, certified Naval Academy guides through the Armel-Leftwich Visitor Center. Visitor Center hours are 9-5 March through December and 9-4 January and February. Proceeds from the sale of Visitor Center tours and tax-free merchandise at the Naval Academy Gift Shop benefit the Brigade of Midshipmen. All visitors over the age of 18 must have a valid picture ID.

PACA HOUSE AND GARDEN
186 Prince George St., Annapolis: 410-267-7619
www.annapolis.org
This is one of Annapolis's most impressive restored 18th Century Georgian mansions, built by William Paca, one of the signers of the Declaration of Independence. When built by Paca in 1763–65, it was one of the first five-part Georgian homes in Annapolis. Its style evokes the English country villas of the time.

Paca, a young lawyer who became one of four Declaration of Independence signers from Maryland as well as governor of Maryland from 1782-85, sold the house in 1780. The property changed hands many times in the 19th century, before becoming part of Carvel Hall—one of the city's most popular hotels for much of the 20th century. By 1965, however, it faced demolition.

A group called Historic Annapolis worked with other preservationists to purchase and save the property. Through meticulous restoration, the home has been returned to its distinctive colonial-era state. Museum-quality period furnishings, including Paca family silver and ceramics, fill its rooms.

Visitors can also explore the spectacular two-acre Paca Garden at their leisure with purchase of a combined ticket.

PREBLE HALL
118 Maryland Ave., Annapolis: 410-293-2108
www.usna.edu/Museum
Named for Edward Preble, who is known for his
service in the War of 1812, this place houses the U.S.
Naval Academy Museum on the grounds of the Naval
Academy. The Museum offers two floors of exhibits
about the history of sea power, the development of
the U.S. Navy, and the role of the U.S. Naval
Academy in producing officers capable of leading
America's sailors and marines. Displays combine
historical artifacts with video and audio technology to
bring to life the stories of the men and women who
have served their country at sea. Whether you are a
casual visitor or a student of naval history, you'll find
a visit here memorable. Part of the fun is just being on
the grounds of this history academy.

SANDY POINT STATE PARK
1100 E College Pkwy., Annapolis: 410-974-2149
http://dnr.maryland.gov/publiclands/Pages/southern/s
andypoint.aspx
Boaters love Sandy Point State Park where activities
include boating, crabbing, fishing, swimming, and
windsurfing. The Park also provides a great view of
the Chesapeake Bay Bridge.

SCHOONER WOODWIND
Dock at Marriott
80 Compromise St., Annapolis, 410-263-7837
www.schoonerwoodwind.com
There have two 74-foot ships, *Woodwind* and
Woodwind II, that sail in the summer season up to 4

times daily on 2-hour public tours of the local waterways. They'll let you help out, perhaps even take the helm. Nominal fee includes free water and a snack. Various private tours are also available, as well as sunset cruises and the like.

WORLD WAR 2 MONUMENT
1920 Governor Ritchie Hwy, Annapolis, 800-446-4926
http://dcmemorials.com/index_indiv0003266.htm
Located just north of Annapolis Maryland on State Route 450 at the Naval Academy bridge, the Maryland World War II Memorial is situated in a beautiful park-like setting at what is commonly known as the Ritchie Overlook.

This lasting tribute to the men and women who fought for the principles of freedom, both abroad and at home, recognizes their contributions as well as educate present and future generations about World War II and its impact as the world's greatest military effort to date.

Maryland's World War II Memorial is unique. Visitors will literally walk through history when visiting the four-sided open-air amphitheater surrounded by a 100-foot diameter ring of 48, 9-foot tall, gray granite pillars. These pillars represent the 48 states at the time of the war. The names of 6,454 Marylanders who lost their lives are etched in granite, providing a lasting tribute to their ultimate contributions. Twenty granite stones accented with stainless steel plaques describe wartime milestones and key events, in addition to contributions made by those 288,000 Maryland men and women who served in the military and those who served at home in the fields and in industry. Two 14-foot diameter granite globes depict the location of key battles in the Eastern and Western Hemispheres. A seven-sided stainless steel obelisk, representing Maryland's status as the country's seventh state, is accented by a star which will be illuminated each night.

This memorial is the culmination of a six-year process which began with the installation of a twenty-five member Commission during the administration of Governor William Donald Schaefer. It is comprised largely of veterans who served their country and their communities, many as professionals from numerous fields and as public servants. This dedicated group, along with advisors from private industry and the State, worked tirelessly to bring Maryland's World War II Memorial to fruition.

A world-wide design competition conducted by a seven-member selection panel culminated in March 1997 with the unanimous selection of a design submitted by New York-based architect Secudino Fernandez. In August 1997, Maryland's Board of Public Works awarded a $1.7 million contract to Priceless Industries of Dundalk, Maryland to serve as general contractor for the Memorial. October 1997 marked the official groundbreaking for the Memorial. It is with great pride and a sense of achievement that all those associated with the planning, funding, and construction that we dedicate Maryland's World War II Memorial.

Chapter 7
SHOPPING & SERVICES

ARUNDEL MILLS
www.simon.com/mall/arundel-mills
7000 Arundel Mills Cir., Hanover: 410-540-5100
This is Maryland's largest outlet and value retail
shopping destination with more than 200 indoor
stores, including Coach Factory Store, J.Crew
Factory, Last Call by Neiman Marcus, Saks Fifth
Avenue OFF 5TH, Vince Camuto Outlet, Fossil,
Pink, Lego, The Disney Store and more.

In addition, they sport lots of chain-style eateries like Buffalo Wild Wings, DuClaw Brewing Company, Dave & Buster's, **Medieval Times Dinner & Tournament.**

Cinemark Egyptian 24 Theatres is also here.

Arundel Mills is home to **Maryland Live! Casino**, a gaming and entertainment outfit, and **Rams Head Center Stage**, a 500-seat, state-of-the-art live entertainment venue.

Located at the intersection of the Baltimore Washington Parkway and Rte.100, 10 miles south of Baltimore, 20 miles north of Washington, D.C. and 2 miles west of the BWI Airport. Hours are 10 a.m. – 9:30 p.m. Mon.-Sat. and 11 a.m. – 7 p.m. on Sunday.

BLUE CRAB ANTIQUES
55 Maryland Ave., Annapolis: 443-949-7055
www.bluecrabantiques.com
Located a block from the Naval Academy, the Maryland State House and the Governor's Mansion. A full-service antique store that sells, buys

and consigns only the highest quality antiques at the lowest possible prices around.

EVERGREEN ANTIQUES
69 Maryland Ave., Annapolis: 410-216-9067
www.facebook.com/EvergreenAntiques
Located in the heart of Annapolis. Items such as glass figurines, rugs, lamps, tables, dressers and chairs.

PENSYLVANIA DUTCH FARMERS MARKET
2472 Solomons Island Rd., Annapolis: 410- 573-0770
www.padutchfarmmarket.com
The Pennsylvania Dutch Farmer's Market, known locally as the "Amish Market", is located in the 290,000 sq ft. Annapolis Harbour Center in historic Annapolis, MD. However, all of the Amish merchants are from Lancaster PA, the heart of PA Dutch Country.

Most of the market's products are made in Lancaster County using traditional PA Dutch recipes that have been handed by the Amish though the generations. You will be able to shop a large quality selection of foods including fresh produce, a variety of salads, a candy store, homemade snacks, desserts, cheeses, chemical free meats, barbequed and fried chicken, foods in bulk and even an ice cream stand featuring Hershey's Ice Cream. Order small portions to eat right away or order large portions to take home.

Our own famous **Dutch Market Restaurant** features a full breakfast, lunch and dinner menu, prepared by Amish cooks, using traditional PA Dutch recipes enriching you with a warm and hearty "homemade" meal.

In addition to the great food selections, **Millwood Furniture** store has a full selection of beautiful handmade solid hardwood furniture for every room of your home.

RE-SAILS
42 Randall St, Annapolis, 410-263-4982
www.resails.com
Unique company creates nautical themed products from old sails. Here you'll find clothes, duffle bags, jackets, and back packs – all with boat numbers on them. The material makes the products strong and long-lasting.

THIRD EYE COMICS
209 Chinquapin Round Rd, Annapolis. 410-897-0322
www.thirdeyecomics.com

Third Eye Comics first opened for business in 2008. Third Eye was born out of a love and lifelong passion shared by husband and wife duo Steve Anderson and Patricia Rabbitt. At the young age of 25, Steve had already spent nearly a decade working in the comic book industry as a manager at the comic shop he grew up shopping with. After spending years saving, and selling his own comic book collection, he and Trish brought life to Third Eye in a tiny, and unconventional little Annapolis storefront.

Now, years later, it's grown into a 5,000 square foot mega-store

Third Eye Comics is an internationally-renowned retailer who has been honored with nominations for the Eisner Spirit of Retailing Award, as well as many other accolades due to our selection and service.

We're known for having one of the largest selections of comic books and graphic novels in the country, as well as a huge variety of merchandise related to comics, geek culture, and gaming culture. In addition to our massive inventory of comics and graphic novels, we stock huge selections of action figures, designer toys, statues, board games / RPGs, collectible card games, a full section of apparel, comic collecting supplies, novelties, and much more.

WEST ANNAPOLIS ANTIQUES
103 Annapolis St., Annapolis: 410-295-1200
NO WEBSITE
Specializes in estate jewelry, sterling, china, crystal and home furnishings.

WESTFIELD ANNAPOLIS
2002 Annapolis Mall, Annapolis: 410-972-4996
www.westfield.com/annapolis/
There are 230 stores in this huge complex, everything
from Abercrombie to Zumiez. (There's a lot in
between the A's and the Z's.)

INDEX

Other Books by the Same Author

Andrew Delaplaine has written in widely varied fields: screenplays, novels (adult and juvenile), travel writing, journalism. His books are available in quality bookstores as well as all online retailers.

Jack Houston
St. Clair Political Thrillers

On Election night, as China and Russia mass soldiers on their common border in preparation for war, there's a tie in the Electoral College that forces the decision for President into the House of Representatives as mandated by the Constitution. The incumbent Republican President, working through his Aide for Congressional

Liaison, uses the Keystone File, which contains dirt on every member of Congress, to blackmail members into supporting the Republican candidate. The action runs from Election Night in November to Inauguration Day on January 20. Jack Houston St. Clair runs a small detective agency in Miami. His father is Florida Governor Sam Houston St. Clair, the Republican candidate. While he tries to help his dad win the election, Jack also gets hired to follow up on some suspicious wire transfers involving drug smugglers, leading him to a sunken narco-sub off Key West that has $65 million in cash in its hull.

The Adventures of Sherlock Holmes IV

In this series, the original Sherlock Holmes's great-great-great grandson solves crimes and mysteries in the present day, working out of the boutique hotel he owns on South Beach.

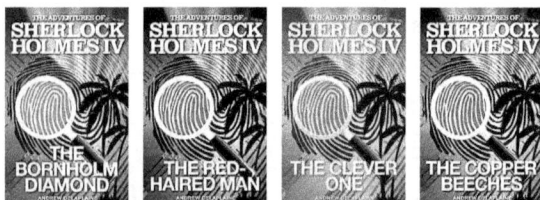

THE BORNHOLM DIAMOND

A mysterious Swedish nobleman requests a meeting to discuss a matter of such serious importance that it may threaten the line of succession in one of the oldest royal houses in Europe.

THE RED-HAIRED MAN

A man with a shock of red hair calls on Sherlock Holmes to solve the mystery of the Red-haired League.

THE CLEVER ONE

A former nun who, while still very devout, has renounced her vows so that she could "find a life, and possibly love, in the real world." She comes to Holmes in hopes that he can find out what happened to the man who promised to marry her, but mysteriously disappeared moments before their wedding.

THE COPPER BEECHES

A nanny reaches out to Sherlock Holmes seeking his advice on whether she should take a new position when her prospective employer has demanded that she cut her hair as part of the job.

THE MAN WITH THE TWISTED LIP

In what seems to be the case of a missing person, Sherlock Holmes navigates his way through a maze of perplexing clues that leads him through a sinister world to a surprising conclusion

THE DEVIL'S FOOT

Holmes's doctor orders him to take a short holiday in Key West, and while there, Holmes is called on to look into a case in which three people involved in a Santería ritual died with no explanation.

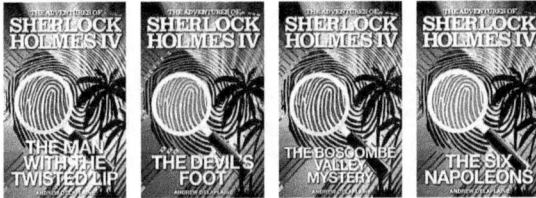

THE BOSCOMBE VALLEY MYSTERY

Sherlock Holmes and Watson are called to a remote area of Florida overlooking Lake Okeechobee to investigate a murder where all the evidence points to the victim's son as the killer. Holmes, however, is not so sure.

THE SIX NAPOLEONS

Inspector Lestrade calls on Holmes to help him figure out why a madman would go around Miami breaking into homes and businesses to destroy cheap busts of the French Emperor. It all seems very insignificant to Holmes—until, of course, a murder occurs.

NOTES